PLEASURES AND TREASURES

FRENCH PORCELAIN

Endpapers: Two original drawings
for Sèvres plates, decorated in
the Chinese style

POR

HUBERT LANDAIS

Translated from the French by ISABEL and FLORENCE MCHUGH

Photographs by E. BOUDOT-LAMOTTE

FRENCH CELAIN

G. P. PUTNAM'S SONS
NEW YORK

Acknowledgments

Plates IV, V, VII, X, XVI and figure 5, 6, 9, 16, 18, 22, 23, 29 and 30 are reproduced by courtesy of the Musée des Arts Décoratifs, Paris
Plates XVII, XVIII, XIX, XX, XXI, XXII, XXIII, XXIV, XXV, XXVII, XXXI, XXXII, XXXIII, and figures 32, 33, 34, 35, 41, 42, 43, 45, 46, 49, 50, 51, 54 and 81 are reproduced by permission of the Musée du Louvre, Paris
Plates I, II, III, VI, VIII, IX, XI, XII, XIII, XIV, XV and figures 7, 8, 10, 12, 13, 14, 15, 17, 19, 21, 24, 25, 26, 27 and 28 appear by permission of the Musée de Saumur
Plates XXVI, XXVIII, XXIX, XXX, XXXIV, and figures 60, 61, 62, 63, 64, 66, 69, 71, 73, 75, 79 and 80 are reproduced by permission of the Musée de Sèvres
Figure 20 appears by courtesy of the Witt Library and figure 38 by courtesy of *The Connoisseur* magazine
Figures 2, 3, 4, 31, 39, 40, 47, 48, 52, 55, 56, 57, 58, 65, 68, 72, 79 and 82 are reproduced by permission of the Victoria and Albert Museum and figures 1, 36, 37, 44, 53, 67 and 77 by courtesy of the Trustees of the Wallace Collection, London
The photographs in the Victoria and Albert Museum were taken by C. H. Cannings, figure 11 by the Archives Photographiques, and figures 1, 36, 37, 44, 53, 67 and 77 by the Wallace Collection
The photographs from the Musée de Saumur were taken by Franceschi and all the other pictures were specially taken for this book by E. Boudot-Lamotte, Paris

My profound gratitude is due to those of my colleagues who have facilitated the writing of this work by their kindly co-operation: Monsieur Verlet, curator-in-chief of the Musée du Louvre; Monsieur Guérin, curator-in-chief of the Musée des Arts Décoratifs; Monsieur Fourest, curator of the Musée National de Céramique de Sévres; Mademoiselle Giacomotti and Monsieur S. Grandjean, assistants at the Musée du Louvre and Mademoiselle Jacob, curator of the Musée de Saumur

1 A Sèvres vase clock of green *oeil-de-perdrix*, mounted in ormolu like so many European or Oriental porcelains

Introduction

THERE ARE MANY POSSIBLE WAYS in which one might set about writing a history of the French porcelains of the eighteenth century. An account of the forms would lead on to an examination of the emergence of the given types of each factory, and would have the advantage of enabling the reader to lay his finger on the prodigious variety of objects produced and at the same time place them in their framework, eighteenth-century France. The connection between porcelain and the goldsmith's art and porcelain and sculpture would thus emerge clearly.

To write a history of the decorations employed would take the would-be historian still farther afield, for how could he make a complete study of those employed at Chantilly, Mennecy, or even Vincennes without going back·to the history of oriental ceramics and their appearance in the curio markets of Europe? Meissen and Tournai—particularly Meissen—should have their place in a study of this kind, side by side with certain potteries which, at the end of the seventeenth and beginning of the eighteenth century, undoubtedly influenced the first porcelain makers.

It has, however, seemed more logical to follow a traditional plan which consists in showing the evolution of the styles and decorations of each manufacture separately, at the same time giving a brief *resumé* of its history. No

2 A water-colour sketch for the centre of a Sèvres plate. Both Sèvres and Vincennes were famous for their multi-coloured bouquets of flowers

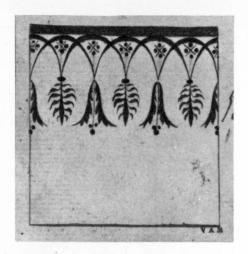

3 A design for a coffee cup, Sèvres, c. 1820, by François Capronnier

doubt it would have been desirable to give more attention to the minor factories which are little known even yet, but I have chosen, rather, to concentrate more on the major centres of production.

I can make no claim to have produced an original work of its kind, for the history of the French porcelains of the eighteenth century has already been written. My purpose is to describe the beauty and charm of this porcelain to a new and wider public and to inspire the amateur collector in his search for fine pieces. To these readers I commend the excellent books which have already done much to make known in France and abroad one of the most original productions of French industry. No work could be written without the help of Chavagnac and Grollier, whose *L'Histoire des Manufactures françaises de Porcelaine* (1906) should by right be cited as a source on every single page of this little book. Their work has served as a source for all the works on the subject written since 1906 in all languages. Of these, the most important are in French Alfassa and Guérin's *La porcelaine française du XVII° au milieu du XIX° siécle* (1930) and G. Fontaine's *La porcelaine française*; and in English, W. B. Honey's *French Porcelain of the 18th century* (1950).

Valuable monographs, of which there are all too few, complement these works and are of great interest to the collector. Those of Milet on Rouen Porcelain (1898), and of Darblay on Mennecy Porcelain (1901) have been drawn on by Chavagnac and Grollier. More recent are those of G. Arnaud d'Agnel on Marseilles Porcelain (1912) and H. Haug on Strasbourg Porcelain (1922), whilst the essential works on Sèvres Porcelain are those of Lechevallier-Chevignard (1908) and by the same author in collaboration with Bourgeois on the Biscuit Porcelains (1914); by Troude (1897) on the forms, by Garnier (undated), and finally, by P. Verlet, S. Grandjean, and M. Brunet (1954). Other monographs, unfortunately unpublished, have formed the subject of theses at the Ecole du Louvre. Some of these have been printed in part as articles in the *Cahiers de la Céramique et des Arts du Feu*, a sumptuous periodical published by *Les Amis de Sèvres*, to which I refer below as *Cahiers*. Among these are Monsieur Grandjean on *Sèvres of the Empire*, Mlle. Ballu on Chantilly, and Mlle. Plinval-Salgues on the factory at the Faubourg Saint-Denis.

The special charm of the French porcelains has attracted many collectors in France and abroad, and public and private collections, often of considerable size, have assembled a great number of pieces of high quality.

In England there is a very fine collection in the Victoria and Albert Museum, whilst the display of Sèvres in the Wallace Collection has no equal in France itself. In America the Kress Foundation has recently given the Metropolitan Museum of Art in New York some really first-class Sèvres pieces. Good, representative collections can also be seen in the Walters Art Gallery in Baltimore, which houses the Hodgkins Porcelains, and in the Huntington Art Gallery of San Marino in California. In France the Musée de Sèvres, the Musée des Arts Décoratifs and the Musée du Louvre form an astoundingly rich national treasury: from these sources most of the illustrations have been taken, together with some pieces from the Lair Collection at the Musée de Saumur. It would have been tempting to include illustrations of the chief masterpieces assembled in Paris, London and New York. My aim has been more modest: basically, I have tried to show a certain number of typical pieces, but without always keeping to the masterpiece plane of the 'unique' pieces. These latter have certainly assured the renown of French manufactures, but the amateur will certainly never meet them outside the show cases of the great museums or in collections not open to the public. And it is to amateur collectors of French porcelain that this book is addressed.

4 Another sketch for a coffee cup by the same artist

9

5 A silver-mounted box decorated with green flowers from Saint-Cloud, one of the earliest French factories

CHAPTER ONE

The First French Porcelains

THE FIRST PORCELAINS to be found in the West are imported porcelains. We do not know exactly what is meant by the term *'porcelaine'* which we sometimes come upon in late fifteenth-century inventories, but it was, nevertheless, from the end of that century that true porcelain, as opposed to sea-shell or mother-of-pearl (to which the name was first applied), began to intrigue lovers of the exotic. In Portugal and Venice people began to speculate about the nature and composition of those mysterious treasures for whose possession the great collectors and curio lovers of those days competed. Francis I, the Emperor Charles V, the Medicis, all possessed porcelains which we find in their inventories and which we have every reason to assume were imported. For it was possible to send orders even to the Far East through Portuguese travellers or Dutch merchants in those far-off days. Historians of Chinese ceramics frequently mention the first Ming porcelains made for King Manoel of Portugal, or for the Emperor Charles V, who was the possessor of the earliest surviving dinner-service decorated with armorial bearings which has come down to us.

The success of oriental porcelain was considerable, and the sole explanation of the birth of European porcelain in general and French porcelain in particular is the passionate desire that existed in Europe to discover the

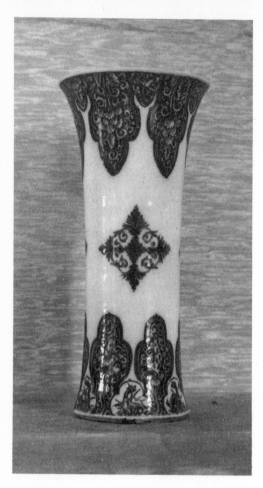

6 The earliest European porcelain was made at the end of the seventeenth century in imitation of imported Oriental ceramics and was generally unsigned; an early French vase

secrets of the manufacture of those marvellous translucent ceramics sold in the great markets of the East. The most celebrated examples of the earliest efforts to make porcelain in Europe are the famous Medici porcelains, which were made in the sixteenth century under the aegis of the Grand Dukes of Tuscany.

It is important to remember that porcelain is divided into two classes, soft paste and hard paste. Soft paste is a combination of materials, more or less vitrified after heating, other substances —such as white clay— were added to make the paste opaque. Hard porcelain is made of china-stone and kaolin or china clay. After the original firings of soft paste, the glaze —generally very fusible glass— was applied at a lower temperature. In hard paste the body and glaze are fired simultaneously in a fierce heat, causing complete incorporation of the two. Thus soft paste is more porous and stains by use. If broken, one can easily distinguish between them; soft paste has an irregular, granular texture, while hard paste has a smooth white surface.

The early potters' difficulty was their ignorance of the composition of the oriental porcelains. These porcelains, as everyone knows nowadays, are made of kaolin, a white infusible clay at that time unknown to the West, mixed with a feldspar or white crystalline mineral called petuntse. By dint of many experiments and much patience, experts in all countries discovered certain facts which to us today seem elementary. In Germany Walter von Thirnhausen, with the aid of the ceramist Böttger, analysed all the minerals to be found in Saxony, and submitted them to very high temperatures. Actually, his aim was not to discover kaolin but to find out how to make silver synthetically, while Böttger had only been taken into the service of Augustus the Strong because he claimed that he could make gold. But instead of gold or silver this collaboration between Thirnhausen and Böttger resulted in the first hard-paste porcelains to be produced in Europe.

The French physicist Réaumur also applied himself intensively, with more system but less lucky results, to experiments in porcelain-making. He set down his findings in a series of memoranda which he read to the Académie des Sciences in 1727, 1729 and 1739. Lacking the elementary raw materials, he imagined he could obtain porcelain by devitrifying at high temperatures objects made of glass. These '*porcelaines de Réaumur*' were never made on an industrial scale, and must not be confused with the 'glass porcelains' dear to certain Paris and provincial glass manufacturers, who asserted that they were equal to the porcelains of China. Perrot of Orléans (d. 1709) is one of the chief names associated with this product.

If European potters were ignorant of kaolin and its use, they had a perfect knowledge of pottery, and it was to perfecting and refining the pastes used for making pottery, especially fine pottery, that the first *porcelainiers* applied themselves. Hence it is not surprising to learn that each centre had its own secret processes, its own measures, its particular skills, but also its *ratages* (misfires), which always prevented the so-called soft paste porcelains from being manufactured on a really industrial scale. Being works of art, they were not made in '*série*' or batches, but always bear the mark of an interesting experiment, a quest for perfection.

The oriental style of decoration was obviously the most prized by early porcelain makers, who created exact copies, free copies, European interpretations—such were the stages of development through which passed the 'Chinese' or 'Japanese' porcelains, which saw the light at Saint-Cloud, Mennecy and Chantilly. A few quotations from contemporary documents suffice to show how important for the industry was this urge to imitate. The letters-patent granted in 1673 to Louis Poterat

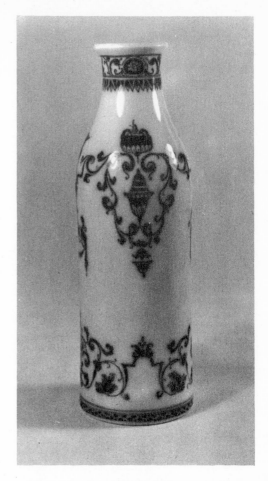

7 This vase is probably from Rouen, a pottery centre which turned to porcelain manufacture in the late seventeenth century. Its blue and white design is taken from Rouen pottery

8 This mustard-pot bears the very rare mark A P, nowadays generally attributed to Rouen, *c*. 1690

9 A cup and saucer attributed to Louis Poterat, who received a licence in 1673 to manufacture at Rouen

10 An early eighteenth-century wine cooler, bearing the sun mark of Saint-Cloud

authorizing him to manufacture porcelains simultaneously with pottery in his factory at Rouen, state that the applicant 'has found the secret of making the true porcelain of China' and that he intends to make 'all sorts of table ware, pots and vases of porcelain similar to that of China'. When M. de Pontchartrain, the Comptroller of Finances, enquired anxiously in 1694 whether the Poterat family 'have also got the secret of making porcelain', the Governor of Rouen replied in the affirmative. Similarly, the patent granted to the children of Chicaneau, potter, of Saint-Cloud, stresses the 'secret' discovered by the latter of 'making true porcelain' and the experiment which had produced 'pieces almost as perfect as the porcelains of China and India...'. At Chantilly the Prince de Condé assembled an important collection of oriental porcelains expressly intended for imitation. He used to amuse himself by mixing pieces of Chantilly among his oriental porcelains and setting his visitors guessing.

Sometimes—at Mennecy and Vincennes for example—efforts were made, but only indirectly, to break the virtual monopoly of the oriental style. The Dubois brothers also, on setting up at Vincennes, undertook to manufacture porcelains 'in the Saxon fashion, painted and gilded, of the human form'. But the Meissen manufacturers themselves were imitating oriental porcelain. At this period manufacturers everywhere were trying their utmost, by every means in their power, honest or otherwise, to penetrate the secrets which were beginning to make the hard porcelains of Saxony famous.

These experiments were extremely costly. In fact, many potters were ruined in trying to change over from pottery to porcelain. Some experimental production, for instance that of the Poterats at Rouen and the Dorez at Lills, was the work of individuals, but the majority of conceren could only carry on thanks to the patronage of the great.

I Typical of
the first por-
celain produc-
ed in France:
a blue and
white vase in
imitation of
Far Eastern
porcelain, pro-
bably made in
Rouen, *c.* 1690

Private experimenters, moreover, took care to enlist the protection of the public powers and to obtain monopolies which enabled them to dispose of their merchandise without competition. The Poterats, for example, obtained the exclusive right to manufacture porcelain for the whole of Normandy; the widow and heirs of Pierre Chicaneau, the potter of Saint-Cloud, obtained some years later (1702) a similar licence authorizing them to set up anywhere that seemed good to them, 'excepting within the town and district of Rouen', one centre of several centres for their factory.

Actually, decrees of the Royal Council and even express prohibitions were not always put into operation, and the mere personality of the manufacturers' patrons prevented really effective action being taken against them. Among those patrons who took a passionate interest in these experiments in 'applied chemistry' were the greatest names in the kingdom. The King himself and Madame de Pompadour were the protectors of the Vincennes-Sèvres industry after Orry de Fulvi and Machault the Comptroller-General of Finances, whilst Monsieur, the King's brother, intervened personally to obtain a monopoly for Saint-Cloud; Chantilly's development was due to the patronage of the Prince de Condé, Mennecy's to the Duc de Villeroy, Sceaux to that of the Duchesse de Maine. Each manufacturer strove his utmost to produce work of the highest quality, to discover or steal the secrets of others, and to entice away their craftsmen and secure them for themselves. The less scrupulous of these artists benefited substantially by cashing in on this state of affairs.

A recent article in *Cahiers de la Céramique et des Arts du Feu, 10,* has drawn attention to the curious career of

12 An egg-cup from Saint-Cloud, *c.* 1730

11 *Le Déjeuner* by François Boucher shows some elegant coffee cups and a sugar basin in use at the time they were made. This family, however, preferred a silver coffee pot to a porcelain one

20

II A dressing-table pot made *c.* 1710, bearing the sun mark of Saint-Cloud

III Of the same period as the pot opposite; a sugar sifter from Saint-Cloud

13 After about 1724 the pieces manufactured at Saint-Cloud became more varied: a spice box made *c.* 1730

two of these pioneer craftsmen, the brothers Robert and Gilles Dubois.

Gilles began at the Faubourg Saint-Antoine, went over to Chantilly in 1730, then in turn to Valenciennes, Saint-Amant, Tournai and Sèvres, and finally to Sceaux. The elder brother, Robert, seems to have begun at Chantilly, passed on to Saint-Amant, then to Tournai, and finally back once more to Chantilly. A curious career, certainly, but in the course of it he did not escape disputes with the public authorities, who tried to ensure respect for monopolies and for the jealously guarded secrets of the trade.

Researchers, patrons, absconding workers—these were the people responsible for the astounding development of the porcelains of France during the eighteenth century; the history of this development is equally remarkable.

14 A cup and saucer made at Saint-Cloud, c. 1740 in imitation of *blanc de Chine*, with a pineapple pattern in relief

Who made the first soft paste French porcelains? The available documents supply an answer, at least in outline, to the question. Of these documents the first in date (1664) is a patent granted to one Claude Révérend, potter, of Paris, who boasted that he was able to '*contrefaire la porcelaine aussi belle et plus belle que celle qui vient des Indes orientales*' ('reproduce porcelain as beautiful as, or more beautiful than that which comes from the Eastern Indies'). We do not know who exactly this Révérend was, but it is probable (see especially H. P. Fourest, *Cahiers, 16*) that he was merely a charlatan who never made porcelain himself.

If we eliminate Révérend it would seem that it is to Edme Poterat, potter of Rouen, that credit is due for the discovery of how to make soft-paste French porcelain, at a date difficult to determine. At any rate we know that in 1673 Louis, son of Edme, obtained a licence permitting him to manufactured 'porcelains and pottery in the fashion of Holland'. The patent was to be renewed for thirty

IV A cup and saucer decorated in the Japanese style known as Imari, made at Saint-Cloud, *c.* 1740

V A bowl with Imari decoration, of the same period as the cup and saucer, also from Saint-Cloud

years in 1677. Michel Poterat continued the work of his brother, but his products were inferior to those of Louis, or at least so it would seem if we are to believe the account of d'Ormesson, who mentions Révérend also.

At Saint-Cloud the first porcelains appeared a little later, but likewise at a date difficult to determine exactly. According to a statement made by the heirs of Pierre Chicaneau in 1702, the latter, who must have died prior to 1678, had made 'several experiments in various materials', which had enabled him to find the secret of porcelain-making, a secret transmitted to and used by his heirs.

The *Dictionnaire Universel* of Savary de Brûlons, published in 1723, indicates moreover that such manufacture had been going on 'for the past fifteen or twenty years' (this would mean from about 1703) at Passy; this factory is placed by the author in question in the same category as the one at Saint-Cloud.

To these first factories may be added the one founded at Lille by Barthélémy Dorez, who received his licence in 1711. This concern appears to have lasted until about 1730.

Such is the information to be gleaned from the source documents. An examination of the existing pieces themselves and of their marks does not permit indubitable attribution in every case.

ROUEN PORCELAIN: One thing is certain: the first porcelains nearly always present forms taken from the art of the gold and silversmiths—simple shapes such as vases, cups without handles, saucers, some with gadroons, some not. Handles, being difficult to affix, are eliminated, complicated shapes are avoided. These pieces are generally

16 Saint-Cloud produced numerous handles for walking sticks

15 A white wine cooler with a pattern of foliage in relief, Saint-Cloud, *c.* 1740

VI The blue and white of Saint-Cloud's
early products gradually gave way to
more varied decoration

VII (*left*) A cup and saucer and (*above*) a plate decorated at Saint-Cloud in the oriental style, *c.* 1740

17 Among the earliest Chantilly pieces are those in blue and white, imitations of Rouen and Chantilly or direct copies of the Japanese, such as this small bowl

decorated with blue and white designs of lambrequins (loops), apparently imitated from pottery, or a design ' *a la Bérain*' in the same tone. As a rule these first porcelains are not signed; sometimes, however, they bear indecipherable *graffiti* in blue meant to imitate or counterfeit oriental marks. The vase reproduced in plate I bears a mark of this kind. Chavagnac and Grollier point out that it is not unlike the mark used by the Rouen potter Levavasseur on his wares. Unless one admits a very pronounced archaism, however, the date that they suggest (1743) appears, to say the least, difficult to admit.

A small number of very rare and highly prized pieces bear the monogram A P accompanied by a star or a rowel. This mark, sometimes read as '*A Passy*', is more generally attributed to Rouen. Most of these pieces are decorated in a design of blue and white taken from Rouen pottery. A mustard-pot in the Musée de Sèvres actually bears the coat of arms of Asselin de Villequier, a device to be found on Rouen pottery. Even if the P of the monogram in question can be taken to refer to Poterat, an explanation for the A has yet to be found. Therefore, the attribution of the mustard-pot to Rouen is credible.

Moreover, a number of pieces, all in blue and white [plate I], have been attributed to the Poterat family. The decoration of a vase in the Musée de Sèvres, a rat under a pot of flowers—*Pot-et-rat*—is sometimes interpreted as a pictorial signature of the artist. This vase also shows birds (swans?) very similar to those shown in plate I. In the Rouen pieces the quality of the paste and of the glaze is very variable. This factory appears to have produced much experimental work which apparently it was not possible to continue systematically.

SAINT-CLOUD: At this factory Chicaneau and his heirs began by imitating the Rouen work. In some cases the imitation is so close that one wonders whether the two

30

18 Chantilly porcelain has a delicate and exotic air. Its early Oriental style became mingled with European motifs and produced many charming pieces such as this teapot, in which the European storks have a decidedly Chinese appearance

factories may not have had some definite interrelation at the beginning, such as exchange of secrets or of craftsmen, or some other connections. Whatever it may have been, the widow of Chicaneau, who in 1679 married Charles Trou (*d.* 1696), appears to have possessed, together with this second husband, certain well-tried formulae which enabled the factory to expand to such an extent that it could meet the demand of its clientele regularly, as Rouen could never do.

From the grant of the patent to Saint-Cloud in 1702 until 1722 the Chicaneaus and the Trous managed the concern together, the real proprietors being the Chicaneau family, who owned the secrets of their ancestor. From 1742 or 1743 until his death in 1746 Henri Trou—generally called Henri Trou II to distinguish him from his father—managed the factory alone. He was succeeded by his son, but the business went so badly after this that the factory ceased production in 1766.

Some members of the Chicaneau family were to be found in Paris too, where one Jean-Baptiste had owned a shop since 1700 'for the sale of their porcelains', near the Place des Victoires. No doubt he also sold pottery there. The aunt, Marie Moreau, went off to found a factory in the Rue de la Ville-l'Evêque. It is practically impossible to distinguish the products of this factory from those of Saint-Cloud. After the death of Marie Moreau in 1743 Trou bought her factory. The mark used by this 'branch' of Saint-Cloud is C. M., *i.e.*, Chicaneau-Moreau.

The marks of Saint-Cloud itself are well known. A document of 1696 provides that each piece 'shall be marked with a fleur-de-lis or a sun'. This plan does not seem to have been followed. Nevertheless one cup marked with the fleur-de-lis is known (Musée de Sèvres) and so are a great many pieces marked with a sun, generally

VIII A container for *pot pourri*, made at Saint-Cloud *c.* 1740

19 A Chantilly plate decorated with flowers, a ladybird, a moth, a fly and a dragonfly, *c.* 1750

executed in blue and white. The Musée de Sèvres also possesses a vase in the Grollier Collection marked S. C., which can probably be attributed to Pierre Chicaneau about 1677. The mark of the sun (borne by the pieces illustrated in figure 10 and plate II) has been attributed by Chavagnac and Grollier to the early Chicaneau-Trou partnership of 1696 to about 1724. This was followed by the mark $S_T C$ signifying Saint-Cloud-Trou, which seems to be that of the manufacture from 1724 to 1766. A letter frequently accompanies this sigil (impressed mark), which is printed in blue or red or sometimes simply impressed.

The pieces bearing this last mark are infinitely more varied than the preceding ones. This second flowering of Saint-Cloud has been attributed to the personality of Trou, and also to the personal interest of the Regent, Philippe, Duc d'Orléans, who is said to have confided personally to Trou in 1722 'a new secret' which enabled the latter to perfect his porcelain.

Other innovations, doubtless of earlier date than this 'revelation' of the Regent, were evidently put into practice at Saint-Cloud. The hypothesis has recently been expressed by H.P. Fourest, in his article in *Cahiers de la Céramique et des Arts du Feu, 10*, that some polychrome pieces, unmarked but similar in style to the works executed in blue and white, were produced at Saint-Cloud at the end of the seventeenth century. These exceedingly rare pieces would appear, then, to be the first polychrome porcelains attempted in France. The decoration was applied at a second firing (*au petit feu*).

Be that as it may, the decoration in blue and white is not likely to have been abandoned overnight, but disappeared gradually, giving place to more varied decoration: Chinese white set off by a pattern of raised branches or fruits in relief [figure 14]; imitations of Chinese porcelains of the *Famille verte* style, or of Japanese porcelains of

20 A French engraving showing a banquet in progress at the Spanish Embassy in Paris in 1707. At functions of this kind large table services were needed and the factories often received enormous orders from kings and princes

the style known as Imari [plates IV, V]. The shapes continue to be inspired by the goldsmith's art. Numerous pieces, notably knicknacks representing rockwork, with or without a statuette, and sometimes bearing a bust or a raised pattern of foliage, made the fortune of Saint-Cloud. Certain rather rare pieces have a yellow ground [plate VII]. Others, decorated in oriental designs, are not unlike the products of Meissen and Chantilly. Statuettes, generally representing Chinamen, are to be found in the best collections. Numerous boxes, sometimes silver-mounted [figure 5], and knobs for walking-sticks [figure 16], complete the brief list of the objects produced at Saint-Cloud.

LILLE: This porcelain is less well known. Pieces decorated in blue and white, sometimes bearing the mark D for Dorez and sometimes L for Lille, are generally attributed to that factory. Chavagnac and Grollier suggest that pieces marked with the letters J and B interlaced should be regarded as Lille porcelain.

21 The making of purely European pieces began at Chantilly c. 1760: this wine cooler has a faintly Oriental air about its flowers

22 A lifelike bird from the
Mennecy factory, *c.* 1775

CHAPTER TWO

The Soft-paste Porcelain Factories

CHANTILLY: If one had to choose a word which would describe most accurately at least the first products of Chantilly, the word 'exotic' would inevitably spring to mind. Apart from the very first pieces, on which the colours were burned in at a very high temperature or painted on with strokes more varied than a better technique would have employed, the majority of the pieces from this factory are stamped with an oriental character at once delicate and picturesque, which always charms and is never monotonous. The glaze, which is of tin basis and very fine, enhances the quality of the objects manufactured. The very rare pieces in blue and white, imitations of Rouen and Saint-Cloud or direct copies of Japanese porcelains, are undoubtedly to be placed among the earliest products of Chantilly.

The exoticism of Chantilly can be clearly traced to the founders of the factory, who managed to create a style which held its own there for a long time. Mademoiselle Ballu, in her able essay in *Cahiers de la Céramique et des Arts du Feu, 11,* has thrown light on the influence of the earliest designers and the evolution of the style.

The first impulse seems to have come from the Duc de Bourbon, a curious character, who had occupied his enforced exile by collecting oriental porcelain (of which the inventory after his death in 1740 listed two thousand pieces) and applying himself to research and experiments which definitely resulted in the creation of the factory. It seems, however, that this would not have come to pass through the Duke's efforts alone, for the real founder of Chantilly was Cicaire Cirou, Sieur de Rieux, whose early background is unknown to us. It was to him that the patent of 1735 was granted, after he had been manufacturing porcelain for ten years. He ran the factory until 1751.

A third person, the Sieur Fraisse, also appears to have played an important role. From 1732 or earlier he was the artist employed regularly by the Duke to make from the latter's collections of oriental ceramics, fabrics and other objects the drawings which served as models for the porcelain makers. His *Recueil des Dessins Chinois* was published in 1737.

The evolution of the styles which these three persons succeeded in impressing on Chantilly may be traced more or less by the existing pieces. First, there are the rare copies of oriental pieces, slavishly exact in form and decoration; then, less rare, the pieces with designs or elements of oriental designs so skilfully transposed by the hand of the Western artist that one hardly perceives that they are so transposed; and finally, the juxtaposition of decorations taken from different sources, which emphasises perhaps still more the character of exoticism already mentioned. There is, however, one dominant feature worthy of note: the influence of that style incorrectly called Korean but definitely inspired by those porcelains known as Kakiemon (after a family of Chinese porcelain makers), of which the Duke doubtless possessed many specimens. The designs thus borrowed, and very often re-used, occur with increasing frequency; for instance the hedgerow design [plate IX], the factory design, the squirrel design and the wheatsheaf design. The shapes themselves are sometimes strange, but always original

23 A wine cooler from Chantilly, *c.* 1750-55, decorated in the *chinoiserie* style that was so popular in the eighteenth century in all the decorative arts

and charming. They often recall those of oriental porcelain whilst yet remaining suitable in a European setting.

Little by little the copying becomes more free; the Chinamen who adorn vases, sugar-basins, buckets [figure 23] and flower-pots, become more Western: the European style enters Chantilly. The flowers of European gardens, notably pansies, which Mademoiselle Ballu notes 'are nowhere so beautiful as at Chantilly', begin to mingle with the exotic ones; European animals and birds (notably storks), take on an amusingly Chinese air, and fraternize with strange creatures drawn from life in the Duke's menagerie [figure 18]. According to Mlle. Ballu, this evolution took place between 1730 and 1760.

By the latter date the Duc de Bourbon had been dead twenty years; Cicaire Cirou had given up the management of the factory ten years before. He had been replaced in 1752 by Buquet de Montvallier, who acted in partnership with Roussière at first, but in 1754 became sole director and remained so until 1757. Buquet de Montvallier continued the manufacture carried on by his predecessor. After him there came a difficult period in the administration of the factory. His successor, Peyrard, former *concierge* at the Château, did not really become titular proprietor until 1760, in which position he was to remain until 1776. His successors from 1776 until 1781 were a husband and wife named Gravant. Louis-François Gravant was the son of François Gravant, a companion of the Dubois brothers who, in 1738, had followed the latter to Vincennes. Gravant was succeeded in 1781 by Antheaume de Surval, from whom the factory passed, in 1792, to the Englishman, Potter. Production ceased at the beginning of the nineteenth century.

It was in the time of Peyrard (1760-76) and his immediate successors that the making of purely European pieces was begun. From then onwards Chantilly porcelain no longer had the originality of the preceding periods.

24 A cup and saucer decorated with a sprig of flowers, made at Chantilly in the time of Peyrard's ownership of the factory, 1760-76, when purely European pieces were introduced

25 A plate, sugar bowl and sugar spoon, part of a Mennecy table service, *c.* 1775

26 A wine cooler from the Villers-Cotterets table service, made at Chantilly *c.* 1775

'Louis Quinze' shapes were introduced at the same time as floral decorations (sometimes in imitation of Meissen), landscapes, love scenes after Boucher, or table services decorated with sprays [plate XI] or with garlands such as the service in blue and white, emblazoned with the arms of the Duc d'Orléans [figures 26 and 27]. Among the other services the most celebrated are the one emblazoned with the arms of the Prince de Condé; and the one known as '*de la Ménagerie*'. The rims are sometimes decorated with basketwork designs which are not peculiar to Chantilly. Statuettes too continued to be fairly numerous.

The marks of Chantilly have been studied, but have not always yielded up much information. The essential mark is the hunter's horn, which is sometimes in red, sometimes in blue, and sometimes incised. This horn is often accompanied by letters, of which we do not know the meaning, and sometimes by dates.

MENNECY, BOURG-LA-REINE AND SCEAUX: The origins of Mennecy porcelain, better called Villeroy, would seem to be traceable to Paris, where a factory was started about 1734 in the Rue de Charonne under the management of Sieur François Barbin. No doubt it was the granting of the licence to Sèvres in 1745 that stopped the activity of this factory. It was about this time (1748) that Barbin 'had been obliged to solicit the Duc de Villeroy for a site on his lands of Villeroy, that he might work there under the protection of the (ducal) court'.

According to Chavagnac and Grollier, it is possible that Barbin may have been running a pottery at Villeroy prior to 1748 whilst continuing his porcelain manufacture at the Rue de Charonne in Paris. However that may be, even if François himself lived in the Château de Villeroy, he started his factory in the nearby town of Mennecy. J. B. Barbin became his father's partner in 1755, and sole proprietor in 1764. After him one may regard the history of Mennecy proper as ended. In 1768 Jospeh Jullien and Symphorien Jacques, the lessees of the Sceaux factory, were also running the Mennecy factory, and up to 1772 were able to call themselves 'maîtres des manufactures de Villeroy et de Sceaux'. Jullien and Jacques left Sceaux in 1772 and Mennecy the following year to go to Bourg-la-Reine, where the Comte d'Eu awaited them. The new centre at Bourg-la-Reine, which does not seem to have prospered greatly, remained in production until 1804.

The marks of Mennecy are the letters D. V., which are interpreted as standing for 'Duché de Villeroy' or 'Duc de Villeroy'. These letters are occasionally in red or in black, but more often incised or in blue. The incised mark B.R. is that of Bourg-la-Reine.

The artistic importance of the Mennecy porcelains is definitely less than that of Chantilly. Not that the pieces produced are of inferior quality—some of them are very fine indeed—but few original creations saw the light under the patronage of the Duc de Villeroy. There was a great deal of imitation of Mennecy and Vincennes, whilst Chantilly, Saint-Cloud and Meissen also exercised a powerful attraction which influenced decisively the productions of the new factory.

Among these imitations the first seem to have been of Saint-Cloud porcelain in blue and white, or in Chinese white decorated with raised sprays, or a basketwork design. The raised sprays are sometimes polychrome. The ' Chinese ' decoration, on the other hand, seems to come from Chantilly, which Mennecy imitated sometimes even to the extent of adopting the tin glaze, whilst the pictures and the flowers are often derived from Vincennes or Meissen.

Nevertheless the artists of Mennecy were capable of producing original work. Indeed, one of the Mennecy specialities seems to have been the making of small objects—snuff boxes, sweetmeat boxes, handles of knives,

27 A plate from the Villers-Cotterets service. The arms are those of the Duc d'Orléans

28 *above and opposite*. After 1760 Mennecy porcelain was decorated with landscapes: the basketwork panels on these plates, however, are not peculiar to Mennecy alone

and the *pots à fards* intended for the interior adornment of ladies' dressing-tables, sometimes mounted in gilded bronze or in silver, little candlesticks [plate XIII], etc. These charming creations, often of exquisite taste, are decorated with designs of flowers or birds. The examples of Mennecy porcelain illustrated in this book seem fairly typical in this respect. The little candlestick [plate XIII] belongs to a set of four; the little pots [plate XII] come from a dressing-table set. Their polychrome decoration is extremely fine. The statuettes are sometimes in the Chinese style [plates XIV and XV], sometimes in purely French or European style, an imitation of those which Vincennes, Sèvres and Meissen had brought into fashion.

The table services, on the other hand, are more rare. We show here two plates [figure 28] decorated with multi-coloured landscapes, the decoration of the rims consisting of an alternating design of cut flowers and basketwork. Charming birds of multi-coloured plumage are carried out in relief [figure 22], or are used to lend a touch of gaiety to plates, vases or ewers [figure 29].

Bourg-la-Reine was, as we have seen, only an extension of Mennecy. The decoration does not differ from what we have just seen [plate XVI]. The new factory made a speciality of 'vases, figures, groups, and of everything relating to the service of the table' (*Almanach* of 1789, quoted by Chavagnac and Grollier).

Sceaux, too, had many associations with Mennecy, if only in the period when Jullien and Jacques were running the two works. There was a pottery at Sceaux already, and apparently it was under cover of this that De Bey, who ran it, managed by joining forces with the porcelain maker Chapelle, to start in 1749 a factory which he hoped in vain would put Sèvres, which relied on its patents and monopolies, out of business. Arrests of and lawsuits against artists such as Chanou, who worked for Sceaux and Vincennes at the same time, did not prevent the manufacture from developing, but all the same it remained comparatively limited.

After the death of the Duchesse de Maine (the official protectress of the enterprise) in 1735, the Duc de Penthièvre permitted the experimental work to continue. Chapelle, left alone, let the factory in 1763 to Joseph Jullien and Symphorien Jacques before selling it, in 1772, to Richard Glot, 'equerry and quarter-master of the King's household'.

The decoration of the Sceaux pieces often shows the influence of other manufactures—Saint-Cloud (looped patterns), Chantilly (sprays), Sèvres (landscapes), and also that of the pottery of Sceaux itself: it is certain that some artists worked simultaneously on the decoration of the pottery and the porcelain.

The birds of Sceaux in themselves made the reputation of the factory.

BEFORE EMBARKING ON the history of the most important of all the French manufactures of porcelain, namely, Sèvres, we must say a few words about the other centres of porcelain making. They are not of comparable importance; nevertheless they cannot be completely ignored.

Nothing is known about the porcelains which are said to have been made at Tours by Jean-Baptiste Rousssin, but we are somewhat better informed about the neighbouring manufacture at Orléans. It was founded in 1735 by Dessaut de Romilly, who sold his factory some years later to Gérault d'Areaubert, whose establishment later took the title of *Manufacture royale de porceleyne d'Orléans*. The mark, which was registered with the Governor of Orléans, consists of an O surmounted by a crown, and it is borne by pieces in blue and white in the style of Chantilly, or with floral designs, or multi-coloured. We shall come across Gérault later as a manufacturer of hard paste porcelains; his mark will then be the label which figures in the coat-of-arms of the Orléans family. It is not known whether this mark, which is found on soft porcelains, should be attributed to the same town.

Two little porcelain works, Crépy en Valois, and Etiolles, both near Mennecy, were to prove very short-lived. A passage from the historian Carlier (1764), quoted by Chavagnac and Grollier, states that a project had been formed some years previously, '*d'établir à Villers-Cotterets une manufacture de fayance*'. This project fell through, but was realized instead at Crépy, of which the same historian tells us that 'as yet nothing has come from that factory but porcelain jewellery, snuff-boxes, sugar-basins, impastos and vases of various shapes, but these works are entirely beautiful and of perfect workmanship'. At the same period (1764) they began to work at Crépy on 'the large-scale production of complete table-services and of the principal articles which normally come from a factory of this kind'. The founder of the factory was one of Mennecy's craftsmen, François Gagnepain, who took as his partner a Paris draper, P. Bourgeois, whose task was to dispose of the goods produced. But apparently the Crépy factory did not continue after the death of its founder in 1770.

The Crépy marks are CP, or Crépy written in full, or sometimes the letters DCP, of which the meaning is not clear. The porcelains which bear these marks are for the most part small pieces, little boxes and other things, sometimes decorated with flowers of Mennecy inspiration.

Etiolles, like Crépy, is not far from Mennecy. The factory there was founded by one J. B. Monier and his partner Pellevé. The closed initials MP stand for Monier-Pellevé. The mark Etiolles written in full, on the other hand, denotes the hard porcelains of the same factory. Though close to Mennecy, Etiolles was influenced primarily by Saint-Cloud, and its few surviving known and marked pieces are poor imitations of Saint-Cloud porcelains.

29 Mennecy table services are comparatively rare: this ewer is ornamented with brightly-coloured tropical birds

30 A small bowl decorated with sprays of flowers in the style of Chantilly, made at Sceaux *c.* 1760-75

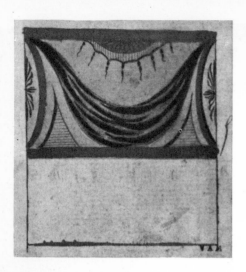

31 An early nineteenth-century design for a Sèvres coffee cup

I have deliberately refrained from including in this review the factory of Tournai, of which the products were, however, very much akin to those of its French competitors. It was probably thanks to the Dubois brothers, mentioned earlier, that Peterink's factory at Tournai got hold of certain secrets, and its wares were widely distributed. In order to counter this competition in northern France, the States of Artois subsidized the development of the porcelain factory at Arras, founded in 1770 by Joseph-François Boussemart, a porcelain maker from Lille, who was succeeded by the Mademoiselles Delemer. The monogram AR is found on the table-ware, whose decoration is difficult to distinguish from that of Tournai. In spite of having powerful protectors, including the Calonne and Caumartin families, the competition of Tournai proved too strong, and the Arras factory ceased production in 1790.

In the same region, J. B. Fauquez, a potter of Saint-Amand-les-Eaux, applied in 1771 for a licence to start manufacturing soft paste porcelain in addition to his pottery. This licence was refused because the authorities feared that, the town being an open one, Fauquez really meant to import foreign ceramics and mark them with his name. Nevertheless he did actually manufacture porcelains from 1771 to 1778. They are marked with two interlaced F's and the letters SA, and for the most part are monochromes (*camaïeux*) in blues, reds or violets.

None of these factories could aspire to rival that of Sèvres which became, under Royal patronage, the most famous and successful of all.

IX A cup and saucer decorated in the so-called Korean manner, made at Chantilly c. 1750

32 At the beginning, the Vincennes factory concentrated on its competition with Saxony porcelain, and this vase, whose *genre* painting was inspired by Watteau, is 'in the Saxon fashion'

CHAPTER THREE

Vincennes and Sèvres

THE STORY OF THE ORIGIN of the Sèvres manufacture, the success of which was to eclipse that of all its French and foreign rivals with astonishing rapidity, seems suspiciously like a swindle and an abuse of power in high places.

We have already met the brothers Dubois, who deserted from Chantilly. Towards 1740 they succeeded in persuading Orry de Fulvi, whose brother, the Comptroller-General of Finances, had power over all industrial undertakings, to found a porcelain factory. For they asserted that with the secrets they possessed they had every prospect of competing successfully with the other centres of production. Orry de Fulvi succumbed to temptation and undertook to obtain premises for the newcomers, who were subsequently permitted to set up their workshops in the Château de Vincennes, 'in the courtyard of the superintendent of buildings of the said château, where the kitchens had been formerly'.

It appears that the Dubois' experiments were not successful; nevertheless they succeeded in obtaining what nowadays we would call subsidies, both through Orry de Fulvi's influence and from the King himself, who lost ten thousand francs in the business, if we are to believe a report of 1745. Orry de Fulvi got tired of this state of affairs, and in 1744 the Dubois brothers were dismissed. The enterprise was not abandoned, however, because the

X A pot with moulded dragons for handles, Chantilly, *c.* 1750

XI The handle of this sugar basin is formed by a cluster of flowers, Chantilly, *c.* 1755

secret of the Dubois apparently really existed, and one day when they were drunk, so the story goes, it was obtained from them by stealth by one François Gravant, a former grocer of Chantilly, who had previously been a potter.

The year 1745 marks a decisive turn in the fortune of Vincennes, for two important events took place, which were to influence the future. First, Orry de Vignori, brother of Orry de Fulvi, was dismissed and replaced as Comptroller of Finances by Jean-Baptiste Machault, a cultured and enlightened man and a patron of the arts, who from now onwards was to exercise at least some supervision over the enterprise.

In the second place, Charles Adam, who had been at Vincennes since 1741, having succeeded (with the help of Gravant) in formulating and working out a process, asked for and obtained a monopoly forbidding 'any persons, under pain of a fine of three thousand francs, unless it be those who have obtained letters-patent authorizing them to do so, either to set up or to cause to be set up, any establishment for the production of porcelain'. The patent also protected the secrets of the new factory. This patent was to be renewed later (1747) and to result in the closing down of the Rue de Charonne works in 1748, the quarrels with Sceaux, and the arrest of certain artists—Caillat, who was accused of trying to get away to England, the brothers Dubois, Chaponnet who was arrested at Lille on his way to Tournai, and many others.

Under the aegis of Machault, the new Comptroller of Finances, newcomers arrived to complete the reduced staffs. Hellot, a fine chemist, applied himself to perfecting the technique; d'Hults 'chose the shapes and directed the decoration and the painting'. He was assisted by Bachelier who was to become very important later and ultimately to take charge of the sculpture department. Duplessis, a goldsmith by trade, succeeded in adapting

33 A covered dish and plate from Vincennes, *c.* 1750, painted with many coloured flowers. The Rococo curves of its
handles are typical of Louis XV style

XII Three small covered pots which were used on ladies' dressing tables to contain face powders and creams (*pots à fard*), made at Mennecy *c.* 1750

XIII Mennecy produced many small delicate pieces such as this little candlestick, a speciality of the factory

34 Inspired by Boucher and his imitators, the monochrome figures of Cupid in blue or pink which decorate Vincennes porcelain are entirely French in feeling

certain patterns of his trade to porcelain, and himself supervised the fashioning of the pieces. And finally Mathieu, the King's enameller, supervised the painting and gilding. Such was the staff secured by Machault, and these were the men who were to assure the successful 'launching' of Vincennes. At the same time a company was formed with a capital of ninety thousand, three hundred francs to supply the necessary running costs. The administration proper was in the hands of the Sieur Boileau and of Blanchard, who had charge of the stocks and warehouses.

In 1752 Charles Adam left the concern, and it was to Eloi Brichard that a new monopoly, even more exclusive than the previous ones, was granted on the 19th August of that year. Brichard received, in effect, to the exclusion of all competitors, the authorization to manufacture 'every kind of work or piece in porcelain, painted or not painted, gilded or not gilded, smooth or with raised pattern, in sculpture or in flowers', and this for twelve years, with effect from the 1st October 1752. This document also provided for the transfer of the factory 'to the premises which are to be built for it in the village of Sèvres', and the mark which the porcelains were to bear was 'a double L interlaced in the form of a monogram' [see below].

Apparently it was at this period, when the new firm was being formed, that the King reserved to himself one-third of the shares.

The production of the Vincennes foundation was very varied and full of novelties, which were destined to be widely distributed for a very long time after the transfer to Sèvres. The date of the first porcelain of Vincennes is difficult to establish with certainty. The mark of the two interlaced L's was certainly in use prior to 1753, and everyone agrees that the first mark in blue was replaced in 1745 by the same monogram accompanied by a dot:

The letters A, B, C, etc., were not used until later, the letter A signifying 1753, the letter B 1754, the letter C 1755 and so on. The pieces bearing these marks are found in a wide range of forms and decorations.

At the beginning the Vincennes factory appears to have applied itself primarily to justifying in some way the real object of its existence, which was to compete with the porcelain of Saxony. Hence it is not surprising to find vases and other pieces in various forms painted with landscapes 'in the Saxon fashion', genre paintings inspired by Watteau or his imitators of the kind shown on the vase in the Louvre [figure 32], or oriental scenes, Chinese or Japanese, which had been copied by European artists. There are also some rare pieces which received a genuinely oriental decoration taken from Chantilly or Saint-Cloud, or possibly copied direct from pieces imported from China and India. The marvellous multi-coloured bouquets of flowers, for which Vincennes became famous, were also 'in the Saxon fashion'. The wife of Gravant, the supplier of the pastes for the factory, ran the workshop in which these flowers of all kinds were painted. One finds these again at Sèvres; the Medici vase in the Louvre has very typical examples of them.

The designs consisting of cut flowers, wreaths of flowers and birds, which were to be replaced very soon by monochromes in pink [figure 34], or blue [figure 35 and plate XVIII], are more specifically French. Inspired by Boucher, or by other painters in fashion at the time, these little figurines with their rose pink skin are among the most charming creations of Vincennes.

Later the genre paintings were cleverly framed with

35 A jug and basin with a turquoise-coloured rim. The coloured grounds were one of the most original features of Vincennes and Sèvres porcelain right through the eighteenth century

XIV Mennecy produced numerous Chinese statuettes.
This pair were made *c.* 1760

36 The factory marks were stamped on the bottom of every piece, except for some very early work. The mark shown here belongs to the Sèvres vase apposite

gold, always of perfect quality. The gold was supplied to the factory by Frère Hippolyte, a Carmelite of Saint-Martin des Champs, who subsequently sold his secret for three thousand francs in cash and six hundred francs in the form of a pension. 'He's the one who's in charge of the wine, he's very stupid', remarked Hellot the chemist.

The coloured grounds, which were to be one of the most marked original features of the soft-paste porcelain of Vincennes and Sèvres right through the eighteenth century, made their appearance very early, without, however, altogether eliminating the white ground. The Louvre Vase has an azure blue ground marbled with gold [figure 32]. P. Verlet, who has carried out the task of making extracts from the account books of Vincennes (incomplete) and Sèvres (of which we only possess those dating from 1753), points out that at that date 'azure blue, with white or gold, appears to predominate; sky blue only appears at the end of 1753'.

The shapes are extremely varied. The *Day Book* of Lazare Duvaux, the Paris draper who retailed quantities of precious pieces bought at Sèvres, commences in 1749. Chavagnac and Grollier have taken from it all references to Vincennes. It shows clearly that the vases were very much sought after and sold at high prices: there were Vincennes vases with floral designs, vases in the form of boats, vases with handles, Duplessis vases, bucket-shaped vases. The account books of the factory also mention shapes which are often difficult to identify today, such as Medici vases, Pompadour urns, Chantilly vases, Parseval vases, antique urns, fluted vases. Their variety is endless.

The table porcelain is also abundant for the period under review, although it does not compare with the fascinating products of the period which was to follow, the goblets,

37 A flower-shaped vase and pierced cover, *rose de Barry* and apple green, made at Sèvres, *c.* 1758, after the transfer of the manufacture from Vincennes to Sèvres

XVI A mustard-pot from Bourg-la-Reine, *c.* 1775, a factory which was only an extension of Mennecy

sugar-bowls, tea-pots, cups and saucers, fruit dishes, bowls, plates, oil pots, cruets, salt-cellars, egg-cups, mustard-pots, basins, etc.

Verlet also draws attention to the toilette articles—shaving-bowls, rouge pots, sponge boxes, of which a great many examples have been preserved.

Finally, an important place should be accorded to the models of sculpture, of which the first known samples are enamelled statuettes of birds and of single figures or groups. Though it is in a class apart we show here *La Source* [plate XIX] which came to the Louvre with the Thiers Collection. It bears the date 1756 and is undoubtedly the most extraordinary example known and perhaps one of the earliest in date of the *porcelaines de France* to be mounted on gilded bronze (ormolu), as certain Meissen and oriental porcelains had already been. At the time of the transfer to Sèvres these ormolu-mounted porcelain figures, (veritable pieces of furniture which one admires as much for their mounting as for the quality of their paste and decoration), were already in fashion.

Biscuit (unglazed white) porcelain, of which Bachelier claimed the invention, appeared towards the middle of the century and rapidly supplanted the polychrome figures. Sculptors such as Suzanne, Duru, Blondeau [figure 61] worked on these. The biscuit figures re-occur at Sèvres later.

It would not do to leave Vincennes without mentioning, in conclusion, some artists whose marks frequently enable us to identify their work. Mention has already been made of Duplessis; Bachelier; the wife of Gravant; Chaunou, who tried to abscond and whose children and grand-children were later to work for Sèvres; and Caillat, who was also arrested at one time and who possessed the secret of certain colours. The painter Capelle supervised the firing of the colours; his wife, a fan-maker, was employed painting flowers; Chaunou the sculptor came from the factory of the Faubourg Saint-Honoré; Bulidon, also a

38 A pen and ink and water colour sketch for a tureen and dish, probably Sèvres, *c.* 1775, now in the Cooper Union Collection in New York

39 An early nineteenth-century design for a Sèvres coffee cup

sculptor, came from Chantilly; Massue, a gilder, came from Saint-Cloud and like Taillandier was a specialist in floral designs and bouquets; Le Guay, 'painter in blue' and gilder, was a relative of the Chicaneau family—his father had worked at Saint-Cloud. One could go on indefinitely naming these artists, so undeservedly forgotten, to whom the fame of Vincennes porcelain is due, but one can conclude by mentioning only a few more—Dodin, painter of figures, who decorated *La Source* [plate XIX], Vieillard, a landscape painter to whom we owe the little tea service of the Louvre [plate XVIII], Caton, a turner who modelled a charming watering-pot which is in the Musée de Sèvres, Armand, painter of birds and flowers. M. Morel d'Arleux has drawn attention, in his article in *Cahiers de la Céramique et des Arts du Feu, 9*, to the rôle played by Dubuisson, who was taken on in 1752 but went over to Chantilly, where he is said to have copied the landscapes created at Vincennes. Most of these artists were to continue at Sèvres the work begun at Vincennes, and there was no break in the continuity between the two manufactures, for the one was the daughter of the other.

The transfer from Vincennes to Sèvres was decided on, as I have said, in 1753, when the manufacture had taken the title of '*manufacture royale de porcelaine*'. From that time onwards Louis XV began to take a personal interest in the enterprise. No doubt he was influenced in this by Madame de Pompadour, who honoured Vincennes and Sèvres with numerous orders, and had been responsible for the nomination of Machault as Comptroller-General of Finances. The King did not, however, appear in the documents under his own title, and Eloi Brichard, whom Louis XV nominated royal warrant-holder for the supply of gold and silver in 1756 (according to M. Verlet's hypothesis), was only a figurehead: his warrant was revoked on 1st October, 1759. The shareholders were indemnified, and from then onwards the factory of Sèvres really belonged to the King, who undertook to put into it the sum of ninety-six thousand francs annually.

The investment of royal funds inaugurated an intelligent policy of subsidies which was to enable the industry to develop harmoniously and to take first place not only on the French market but on the international one too.

The transfer to Sèvres had been made three years previously, not without some harm. The choice of that village had probably been suggested by Madame de Pompadour, and evil tongues whispered that she had done very well out of the sale of La Diarme, the former mansion of Lully designed by the architect Lindet, which she had acquired and which now became the headquarters. The King himself placed an old glassworks at the disposal of the management for housing the workers.

40 Another design for a Sèvres coffee cup, c. 1810, by Capronnier

The administration remained unchanged. Boileau was manager, and Hellot, Blanchard and Bachelier also retained their positions. Gravant continued to supply the pastes up to 1765; after that the raw material was prepared on the premises. The King was represented by an administrator, Monsieur de Courteilles, up to 1757. After that date the royal control was assured by the minister Bertin.

The most notable of the newcomers was Falconet who had charge of the modelling studio until his departure for Russia in 1766. At the head of the other workshops there were several craftsmen who had risen in the industry—Genet, who had begun in 1752 at twenty-one, became head of the painting department in 1756; Deparis, who had been engaged in 1746, was promoted in 1752 assistant to Duplessis, who from that date superintended the moulds.

For sixteen years, from 1756 to 1772, when he died, Boileau directed the factory with competence and honesty. His period of administration was not however without its troubles—the competition of other makers, staff difficulties. In 1770 his cashier Shonen had to be

41 This Vincennes tray has a white ground with blue and gold decoration and naturalistic garlands of flowers

42 The ribbon pattern came into fashion at Sèvres in 1757. This plate with its green ribbons picked out in gold was made in 1758

dismissed for embezzlement. Eight years later the same thing happened to Parent, Boileau's successor. He was replaced by an honest man, Régnier, who remained in office until the Revolution. As Parent had left the concern in a difficult financial situation, the King decided to entrust the supervision of Sèvres to a State administrator, d'Angiviller, the Director of Public Buildings, who was also a collector and a man of culture.

Among the changes which took place during this new period in the history of the industry, there were the appointments of the chemists Cadet and Desmarets in 1784, and of the Swiss, Hettlinger, as assistant manager in 1785. Duplessis, who from this time devoted his attention to the mounting of porcelains in ormolu (gilded bronze), died in 1783 and was succeeded as mounter by Thomire. From 1774 Boizot directed the sculpture department, where he succeeded Bachelier, who from that date supervised the painting. Lagrenée joined him as assistant in 1785.

The appearance of hard porcelain also caused palpable changes in the internal structure of Sèvres, where two distinct manufactures now began to function—that of soft porcelain directed by Deparis and of hard porcelain with Bolvry at its head. In 1783 there were two hundred and seventy-four persons working there on porcelains of all kinds.

The monopoly of Sèvres was relaxed little by little. If one analyses the decrees issued in 1779, 1784 and 1787 one notes a certain hesitation as to the policy to be followed. The directors of the industry were trying to have their rights enforced and defended; the State administration, on the other hand, owing to various pressures being exercised upon it, was practically shutting its eyes to breaches of the monopoly, and was curbing the zeal of its officials who sought to defend it. Little by little the other factories were allowed to use gilding and colours and from 1766 onwards all were compelled to mark their products with a registered mark. In the third quarter of the century the most serious rivalry came from the manufacturers of hard porcelain. The hesitancy of the administration was due to the fact that in this field there was no longer a 'secret' to protect. Hence the monopoly was now felt to be merely a vexation, an abuse of power. The rival factories took advantage of this uncertainty, lured away Sèvres workers by offers of higher wages, stole its raw materials, particularly gold, and often shamelessly and openly copied the shapes and designs which had been created at Sèvres. From 1787 onwards the only monopoly still reserved to Sèvres was the production of 'pieces with a gold ground or others of great luxury, such as pictures in porcelain, and works of sculpture, whether vases or groups, exceeding eighteen inches in height'.

Owing to its inscription on the Civil List by the Constituent Assembly, Sèvres went through some difficult years during the period of the Revolution. From 1793 liquidation pure and simple seemed inevitable, and the payment by Catherine of Russia of ninety thousand francs which she owed, probably saved the former royal factory and enabled it to survive. Battelier, a member of the National Convention, was appointed State administrator and remained so from 1793 to 1795. He was replaced by a triumvirate of whom one was Hettlinger. In 1800 a new director, Alexandre Brongniart, who was later to reorganize the entire industry and restore Sèvres to its former glory, was nominated. One of his first decisions was to abandon the manufacture of soft-paste porcelains.

THE ROYAL MANUFACTURE: From 1753 Vincennes had borne the title of the '*manufacture royale*', and from 1759 the King was sole proprietor of Sèvres. This fact exercised a considerable influence on the style of certain of the objects manufactured. Louis XV and Louis XVI were not content merely with seeing that the enterprise was

43 A cup and saucer with a similar decoration of green ribbons and gay flowers, Sèvres, 1758

44 A Sèvres inkstand which may have belonged to Madame Adelaïde, aunt of Louis XVI. Two globes surround the crown of France; the terrestrial globe shows a surprisingly modern map of Africa and the Persian Gulf, while the celestial indicates the Bear and Leo

45 The medallions which decorate this Sèvres cup with its unusually deep saucer are green picked out with gold and the trellis-work is violet, 1766

well administered and supervising its management, but also honoured it with numerous orders. They set the tone: favourites, courtiers, great noblemen, general contractors, rich *parvenus*—all became eager to possess Sèvres porcelains of quality, but few of the objects so commissioned could rival those made to the order of the Court. There is a royal style in Sèvres porcelain just as there was a royal style in Gobelin tapestries at the height of the reign of Louis XIV. This style is to be found in numerous pieces. These are always sumptuous, and their shape and design is elaborate and often extraordinary. The history of these porcelains made to royal command has been written by P. Verlet, who has described them in his book, *Sèvres*, as well as in two articles, one on the American collections (*Art Quarterly*, Autumn 1954), the other on the English collections (*Burlington Magazine*, July 1954).

There still exists the inkstand delivered to Versailles in 1760 for Madame de Pompadour (now in the Residenz Museum, Munich), of which the Wallace Collection in London possesses a slightly less ornate version, bearing the portrait of the King and the arms of a daughter of France. The candelabra vases with elephants' heads, of which there are examples (several with rose or green ground) in the Wallace Collection and in the Metropolitan Museum in New York, were bought at very high prices in 1758, 1760 and 1762, by the Prince de Condé, Louis XV and Madame de Pompadour. The Victoria and Albert Museum also possesses some mantelpiece brackets delivered in 1761 and 1762 for Versailles. Vases known as 'de Ferré' or more pleasingly as 'de Fontenoy' were bought by the King in 1760, and are now in the Wallace Collection. Whether they are gifts from the King to the Pompadour or pieces ordered direct by the latter, the quality is always

46 The gilding on this plate was done by Henri-François Vincent in 1775, a Sèvres gilder whose indented mark is often encountered

47 A sketch for a Sèvres cup, *c.* 1820

the same. Though it is difficult to be sure that it is to the beautiful Marquise that we owe the 'Pompadour pink' which is so celebrated and so rare, the inventory made after her death, as published by Cordey, shows the interest which she always took in the *'porcelaines de France'*. These orders from the King, from the Court and from foreign sovereigns, diplomats and noblemen, who also frequently received whole services or single pieces as gifts, contributed to the maintenance of a very high standard of quality.

Louis XVI, like Louis XV, was full of solicitude for 'his' factory. He ordered a service from it which was delivered item by item from 1783 to 1803. The accounts concerning this service were written out and kept up to date by the King himself during his life-time. Each plate cost four hundred and eighty francs. This service still exists, and the greater part of it is in the English Royal collections.

SHAPES, DECORATION AND COLOURS: Although the forms created at Sèvres hardly differed at all from those which had seen the light at Vincennes, it is quite obvious that porcelain-making, like the other arts, followed the general evolution of styles, and that the Louis XV style, which was never extreme, should be followed by the Louis XVI style, which was less exuberant. The decoration of the plates, for example, was somewhat more imaginative, perhaps, in the time of Louis XV, with its wreaths [figure 43], its intertwined motifs, its rock-work prettily disposed along rims with slightly vivacious borders. Under Louis XVI, it became more austere, when it gave place to medallions, sometimes surrounded by gilded garlands suggesting an herbaceous border [figure 46], or framing portraits. The influence of antiquity was evident throughout the 1780's—years which saw new forms created.

The books of the factory have enabled Verlet to establish

with even more certainty than at Vincennes the intro-
duction of new colours and decorations.

It was precisely the gaiety and variety of their colours
which made Sèvres plaques so prized for decorating furniture from 1760 onwards and particularly during the reign
of Louis XVI. How can one fail to be dumbfounded
when one contemplates, for instance, a graceful Louis XV
commode completely covered with porcelain plaques? If
the articles by Carlin or sometimes even those by Joseph,
completely plated with Sèvres plaques, sometimes seem
to us rather garish, the workmanship both of the
ébénisterie and of the porcelain compels our admiration.
Porcelain pictures were even used to cover the walls of
extremely luxurious rooms.

The mounted porcelains to which, as we have said,
Duplessis and Thomire devoted their efforts, also had a
great vogue. They were the forerunners of those technical
marvels, the great vases of enamelled or biscuit (unglazed
white) porcelain of the reign of Louis XVI.

The table services are worthy of special mention here.
The most important of these represent royal orders. We
have already mentioned the service made for Louis XVI,
with royal blue ground decorated with multicoloured
genre paintings; Madame Du Barry's service (1770-71)
decorated with her monogram DB and a pattern of pretty
blue cassolettes. The service ordered by Catherine II of
Russia has a blue ground. It too bears a monogram, that
of the Empress, surmounted by the Imperial crown, and
a decoration consisting of cameos. Among the royal gifts
there is the service sent by Louis XV to the Empress
Maria Theresa in 1758, which has the same decoration
as that shown in figure 42; that of the Elector Palatine
(1760); of the Duchess of Bedford (1763); of the King
of Denmark (1768); the two services belonging to Sweden
(1771 and 1784) and the service sent by Louis XVI to
Francis II in 1777.

48 A sketch for a Sèvres cup, *c.* 1820

49-50 (*Left*) This Sèvres vase with its blue *oeil-de-perdrix* ground is Classical in inspiration with its plain shape and goat-headed handles. (*Above*) A plate from the famous Sèvres table service made for the Hope family of Craighall in 1788, bearing their coat-of-arms and flowers painted by Nicquet, a craftsman who specialised in this work

51 A Sèvres coffee cup with a delicate pattern of birds and foliage on a yellow ground made in 1788

The plate shown in plate XXIV is part of the service of Cardinal Louis de Rohan (1772); the container for washing glasses [plate XXIII] is from the Buffon Service which was delivered item by item to the Comte d'Artois from 1779 to 1784. The service of the Hope family of Craighall [figure 50] was ordered from Sèvres by a merchant of Amsterdam named Lefebure.

These services consist of pieces of all kinds, plates both deep and flat, fruit dishes, containers for washing glasses, wine coolers for bottles and half-bottles, sauce-boats, bowls, being very numerous. When delivered, the Rohan service comprised three hundred and sixty pieces; that of Catherine II is said to have comprised seven hundred and forty-four. As for the price of these services, it too was considerable—the Rohan service cost 20,772 francs, and that of Catherine II 331,217 francs.

THE SCULPTURE: The polychrome sculptures dear to Vincennes were resumed at Sèvres only in exceptional cases, for instance for flowers, of which we find several deliveries still being made. There was the order of 1772 mentioned by Chavagnac and Grollier for the Comtesse de Talmont and consisting of '6 daffodils, 6 syringas, 9 campanulas, 6 narcissi, 6 hyacinths, 3 delphiniums, 3 orange-blossoms, 3 buttercups, 3 little rose buds, and 3 marguerites'. In the same year the Paris draper, Darnaud, bought three hundred and sixty-two flowers.

In contrast to this polychrome work, the biscuit pieces which we saw originating at Vincennes were manufactured in great quantities. The models, which could be ordered in several sizes, were made by La Rue, Suzanne, Fernex, Falconet and Brachard [plate XXV], who took their inspiration from the paintings of Boucher, or sometimes created original compositions of their own which are well worthy of the attention of specialists on sculpture. Reproductions of famous sculptures by Lemoyne, Bou-

chardon or Pajou had a commercial success which has lasted into the present day.

ARTISTS AND THEIR MARKS: The artists of Sèvres are far too little known and would deserve special studies to themselves. Some are known by their marks, which the reader will find easily in the works we have already mentioned, for they are too numerous to be included here.

The majority of the painters mentioned in those writings, and whose marks are known, were painters of flowers such as Catrice, Lebel, Michel, Nicquet [figure 50] or Taillandier, all of whose 'signatures' are met with relative frequency. Among the painters of birds were Aloncle, Chapuis the Elder, Evans [plate XXIII] and Ledoux [plate XX]. The specialists in portraits and genre paintings are more rare. One of the most important of these would seem to have been Asselin, who was later to become 'chef des peintres'. Fallot [plate XXIV] and Levé painted ornaments. Sioux painted borders, Binet and Philippine the Elder, figures. Among the gilders, the sigils (indented marks) most frequently encountered are those of Le Guay, Henri-François Vincent and Boulanger.

The sculptors and makers of moulds are somewhat better known. Lists of them have been made but the impressed marks found on the pieces have not always been given, and they deserve systematic study.

As to the marks of the factory itself during the eighteenth century, these are the same as those of Vincennes: the two interlaced L's accompanying a letter, which denoted the date, run from D=1756 to Z=1777 (W being omitted). After 1776 the letters denoting the date are doubled, from AA denoting 1778 to PP denoting 1793. From the 17th July 1793 to 1800 the mark is RF Sèvres written in majuscule characters.

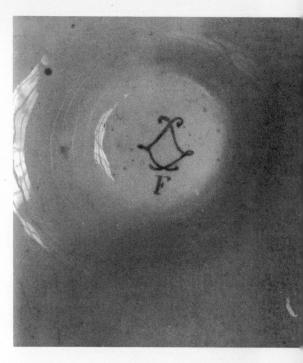

53 The well-known Vincennes and Sèvres mark of two interlaced Ls. The F is a date letter showing that this was made in 1758

52 An early nineteenth-century design for a Chinese plate, painted for the Sèvres works

XVIII A cream jug and sugar basin, part of a Vincennes tea service painted by the landscape artist Vieillard in 1753

XIX *La Source*, one of the earliest statuettes mounted in ormolu, decorated by Dodin, the Vincennes painter, in 1756

54 Classical banners
and a bundle of fasces
are among the emblems
painted on a Sèvres
plate of 1791

CHAPTER FOUR

The Hard-paste Porcelain Factories

55 A nineteenth-century sketch for a Sèvres cup

THE HISTORY OF THE FRENCH hard paste porcelains cannot be separated from that of the soft paste porcelains. The passionate desire of experimenters and of the great nobles whom we have seen at work was to make porcelains like those of the East. Their researches resulted in the first place in the manufacture of products which might be described as intermediate and are among the most original creations of eighteenth-century France; and in the second place, in hard paste porcelain.

The first hard porcelains did not, however, supplant the soft porcelains overnight. During the second half of the century the two manufactures were carried on side by side. Hence it would be quite incorrect to conclude that the porcelain makers of the eighteenth century had made a mistake in abandoning the manufacture of the more artistic soft porcelains in favour of the hard porcelains, which are generally speaking less prized in our day but are technically more perfect. One factory, Saint-Amand, actually continued to manufacture soft porcelains right to the end of the nineteenth century.

The soft porcelains were not without their faults; their preparation was largely empirical and carried great risks. Numerous pieces were spoiled in production and had to be thrown away; the paste frequently got out of shape in the firing. Manufacture on an industrial scale or even

XX This elegant porcelain tub was designed to plant flowers in. The birds were painted by the Sèvres artist Ledoux in 1758

XXI Vases in innumerable shapes were made at Sèvres in the eighteenth century, as the factory's account books show. A vase 'Hollandais', 1758

XXII The discovery of hard-paste porcelain enabled many factories to make more elaborate compositions. This famous great vase of the Louvre, commissioned by Louis XVI in 1783, stands six feet six inches high

in batches was difficult in these conditions. So many factors influenced the cost price that the selling price remained high; hence soft porcelains were always luxury goods which only the privileged could afford.

Finally, even though French factories had been able to enter into competition with Meissen from the middle of the century, one can easily imagine how anxious French porcelain makers were not to allow themselves to be completely left behind on the technical plane, and to succeed in making real, *i.e.*, hard-paste, porcelains.

THE FIRST EXPERIMENTS: On the 28th March 1709 Böttger was able to announce to Augustus the Strong, Elector of Saxony and King of Poland, that he 'had succeeded in obtaining a beautiful white porcelain, capable of taking the most beautiful glazes and all kinds of painted decoration, and which, if not superior to that of the Far East, is at least equal to it'. It had, moreover, 'a hardness superior to that of marble'.

Hard paste European porcelain was born. The first products of the workshop installed near Meissen have for basis a red argil (or clay) called 'bolus'. The kaolin (or Schnorr clay) discovered by Böttger near Schneeberg, enabled him to construct furnaces (1713). Böttger was succeeded by Harold (1719-1731), who was to contribute largely to the success of Meissen porcelain.

The other German factories benefited by the Saxon inventions. It was not only in France that workers deserted, carrying their secrets away with them. Stölzel, who had charge of the furnaces, and Hunger, the enameller, fled in 1717 to Vienna, where they established a rival factory directed by Du Pasquier; the factory at Hoechst was founded about 1750 by a painter from Meissen named Lowenfinck, helped by Viennese technicians, some of whom turn up later at Neudeck, then at Nymphenburg. The Berlin porcelain factory (1752) patronized by Fred-

56 A sketch for a Sèvres cup, *c.* 1820

90

erick II, was also started by deserters from Meissen. In Italy we find another Viennese at the origin of the factory founded by the brothers Vezzi. It was the technicians of Augustus the Strong who were the real founders of the hard porcelain industry not only in Germany but also in Italy.

STRASBOURG: The hard porcelain of France too has a German origin. It was not by chance that the first known samples saw the light in Alsace. Charles-François Hannong, a native of Maestricht, had founded a pipe factory at Strasbourg, in partnership with one Wachenfeld, who had worked at the Anspach porcelain factory. The little factory turned into an important pottery, and in fact a branch was established at Haguenau to avail itself of the German china clays, which were superior to those found on the French side of the Rhine. Charles-François Hannong may have tried to manufacture porcelains, but actually it is to his son Paul, who perhaps imported kaolin from Germany, that credit is due for having introduced hard porcelain manufacture into France. He was helped by former workmen from Meissen and Vienna, notably Roth, Ringler, Lowenfinck and Walter.

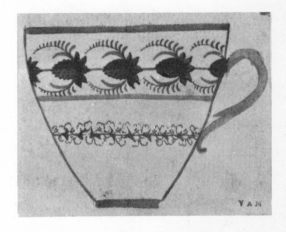

57 A sketch for a Sèvres cup, c. 1820

However, the patent granted to Sèvres in 1745 was a monopoly, and Boileau, who was growing very uneasy, had no intention of allowing dangerous competition to develop. When Hannong came to Paris and applied to Machault for a licence to continue plying his art, he was refused. He then decided to turn to Vincennes and sell his secrets there. Experiments were made, but the essential raw material, kaolin, was lacking, and nothing came of the effort.

Manufacture in France being forbidden him, Hannong decided in 1755 to establish a factory at Frankenthal on the lands of the Elector Palatine, who bought the enterprise in 1761.

91

XXIII This vase for washing glasses at table from the beautiful *Service Buffon* has a picture of a ruff, copied from the works of the celebrated French naturalist Buffon. It was painted by Evans at Sèvres in 1779

XXIV A plate from the table service made at Sèvres in 1772 for Cardinal Louis de Rohan, painted with tropical birds by Fallot

58 An early nineteenth-century sketch for a Sèvres cup

The sons of Charles-François Hannong had an eventful life. Joseph resumed the Strasbourg manufacture, where he was able to make porcelains, the patent of Sèvres issued in 1766 allowing him some partial liberty to do so. But financial difficulties arising from the restrictive duties imposed on his products, and the death of his patron, Cardinal de Rohan, obliged him to close down in 1781. He died in poverty in Munich.

The career of his brother, Pierre-Antoine Hannong, if not more honest, was certainly more adventurous. In 1761 we find him in Paris occupied in selling his secrets to the minister Bertin 'for six thousand francs cash and three thousand francs life annuity'. The aim of his intrigues was to sell to others the secrets already sold to Sèvres. We find him again, this time in partnership with one Sieur Aubiez, in a new enterprise installed at the Château of Vincennes in the former premises of the old royal porcelain works. He was expelled from there in 1770. The following year he founded an establishment in the Saint-Lazare district of Paris, of which little can be traced; he probably also founded the one at Vaux, near Meulan, whilst Lassia, one of his former companions and a Strasbourger like himself, who had discovered his secrets, founded a factory in the Rue de Reuilly. It was to his native Strasbourg that Pierre-Antoine Hannong, that adventurous pioneer of porcelain, returned to end his days. After the death of his brother he had tried to re-establish the family business there.

Let us pause for a moment to examine the nature of the Strasbourg porcelains. M. Haug distinguishes several periods, 'the first from 1751 to 1754, the second from 1771 to 1779, and the third, which consisted merely of the attempt of Pierre-Antoine Hannong to re-establish his brother's industry', from 1783 to 1784. The first pieces produced by Paul Hannong (1751-1754) are difficult to distinguish from those made later on at Frank-

59 This parakeet was copied from
Buffon's drawing on a Sèvres plate.

XXV The Three
Graces, made at
Sèvres, c. 1785. The
biscuit figures
were modelled by
Brachard

enthal. They are for the most part polychrome figurines modelled by Lanz, reproductions in porcelain of the pottery figurines which were responsible for the success and renown of Strasbourg pottery. These pieces are marked PH. From 1771 to 1781 fine pieces are still many and varied. They are frequently copied from other porcelains; table pieces, rare in the previous period, are more plentiful from now onwards. They are monochrome either in blues or reds, decorated *en camaïeu* with stylised flowers, Indian flowers or natural flowers; *genre* paintings of the type reproduced here; Chinese motifs, or wreaths. These pieces are variously marked, sometimes with letters which are believed to refer to the account-books of the factory, which no longer exist. The last period is less productive. No doubt Pierre-Antoine Hannong sometimes contented himself with decorating pieces already manufactured at the time of his brother's bankruptcy.

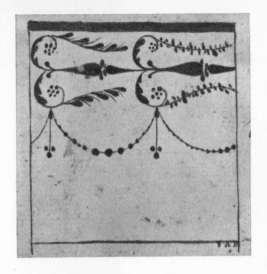

60 A design for a Sèvres coffee cup

NIDERVILLER AND LUNÉVILLE: I have devoted a good deal of attention to Strasbourg because of the importance of the Hannong family in the history of hard porcelain. I shall spend less time on the factory founded in 1765 by the Baron de Beyerlé at Niderviller. Baron de Beyerlé, municipal treasurer of Strasbourg, was interested in ceramics and had already established a pottery at Niderviller in 1754. Like Hannong, he got his kaolin from Germany before he managed to find some in France. Bought by the Comte de Custine in 1780, the factory was then carried on by Lanfrey, who became owner when Custine was guillotined in 1793. The enterprise flourished and in 1789 employed 150 workers. The decoration of the Niderviller pieces is very similar to that of the pottery of the same period and origin—Indian flowers, European flowers, barbels (small sprigs), or landscapes. Imitations of Sèvres are not infrequent. Like all the manufactures of eastern France, Beyerlé and Custine specialized in

97

61 *Le Jeune Suppliant,* a figure modelled in biscuit by Blondeau after Boucher, Sèvres, 1752

polychrome sculptures and biscuit figures. A pupil of Cyflé, Charles Sauvage, otherwise known as Lemire, created numerous models there. Certain other creations do not belong to Niderviller but were made at Luneville by Cyflé himself, who sold his moulds, and probably also his mark, to Lanfrey in 1780. Cyflé, essentially a sculptor, had been specializing since *c.* 1769 in the production of groups of figures in biscuit and in Lorraine clay. The marks of Lunéville are BN (for Beyerlé) and CN or two interlaced C's (for Custine), CFN in monogram form for Lanfrey; and N or Nider for Niderviller. The pieces in Lorraine clay are generally marked with the words in full, and several biscuit figures bear the complete word CYFFLE A LUNEVILLE.

BRANCAS-LAURAGUAIS: The centres of hard porcelain manufacture mentioned above were all in eastern France. Less important, no doubt, on the artistic plane are those pieces which came between about 1764 and 1768 from the Château de Lassay. These porcelains nevertheless have a right to a place apart in the history of hard porcelain, for they are the first pieces made with kaolin quarried on French soil. The Duc de Brancas, Comte de Lauraguais, a member of the Academy of Sciences, devoted himself to experiments in his château. Was it the Duke or Guettard, chemist of the Duc d'Orléans, who discovered a deposit of kaolin near Alençon? No one knows. At any rate it was at Lassay that the discovery was put to use in the period 1764-1768. The production was never on a commercial scale but museums and private collectors possess several table pieces and white medallions of the type shown in figure 66, which bears the monogram BL.

MARSEILLES: Another factory which apparently used Alençon kaolin was that of Robert at Marseilles. At least that is the opinion of both Chavagnac and Grollier on

62 Some of the first hard porcelains to be made in France came from the Hannong brothers' workshops in Strasbourg. La Fontaine's fable of the lion and the fly appears on this cup from Joseph Hannong's factory there

examining the Marseilles paste, which is generally of less beautiful quality than that of the other factories. In a letter sent on 23rd June 1759 by the potter Joseph-Gaspard Robert to the mayor and corporation of Marseilles (as published by Arnaud d'Agnel), Robert explains that he had intended in 1749 to establish a factory at Marseilles but had been deterred at the time because of the opposition he 'had been led to expect on the part of the privileged manufacturers of Vincennes'. He had then abandoned the project and established instead a pottery which was not always prosperous. The object of his letter was to ask the aldermen to intervene on his behalf and obtain for him permission to manufacture porcelains. In 1773 Robert is described as '*marchand de fayence et de porcelaine*'. He then took as partner Jacob Dontu 'maker of porcelain from Berlin in Prussia'. The enterprise seems to have been successful, if we are to judge by the account of a visit Monsieur (the King's brother) paid him on the 27th July 1777. Most of the pieces marked with an R consist of parts of table services with floral decoration, garlands, landscapes, or *genre* paintings, probably showing the influence of Dortu from Berlin [figure 70].

Another Marseilles potter named Honoré Savy experimented in porcelain making from 1759. In 1765 he boasts of having found a green 'superior to that commonly seen' and he asserts that he is 'the only person who knows how to use it'. Sèvres tried to have Savy's formula made known to them, offering him in return permission to set up a porcelain factory in Marseilles.

LIMOGES PORCELAINS: The discovery of kaolin caused an upheaval in the French porcelain industry. The circumstances of this discovery still remain, if not mysterious, at least legendary. I have discussed how kaolin, discovered near Alençon, was used at Lassay. A report by Guettard, who is said to have discovered this deposit, read at the

63 A saucer from Joseph Hannong's factory at Strasbourg

64 A plate from Niderviller, another of the hard paste porcelain factories of eastern France

65 A design for a Sèvres plate in
the Japanese manner: nineteenth century

Academy of Sciences on the 13th November 1765, speaks of kaolin discovered 'in the Limoges district'. So it might have been in 1765, and not in 1768, that the deposit at Saint-Yrieix was brought to light, no doubt by chance. However that may be, it was not until 1768 that the business assumed serious proportions. It is probably to a surgeon named Darnet, living at Saint-Yrieix, that credit is due for the precious find. An apothecary named Villaris from Bordeaux appears to have played a curious rôle as intermediary. It was with him that Macquer, the successor of Hellot at Sèvres, dealt, and it was Villaris also who was charged later with the task of negotiating, on behalf of the King, for the right to exploit a deposit belonging to a lady of Montet. Locally, Darnet himself was entrusted with the quarrying and the initial purification of the mineral.

Other quarries were bought later, whilst yet other deposits besides the royal concession were worked by individuals. By 1769 it was possible to present to the King at Versailles Sèvres pieces made of hard porcelain. The experiments continued for more than ten years, and from 1772 onwards hard porcelain was manufactured at Sèvres side by side with soft.

This combination was favourable, from now on, to amateur and experimental makers of porcelain. There was no longer, properly speaking, any 'secret' in its manufacture, nor any further difficulty in procuring kaolin. Moreover the monopoly of Sèvres was now relaxed. All these factors explain the blossoming forth of factories, both great and small, which the great personages of the day continued to patronise.

The Comte d'Artois, the Comte de Provence, the Duc d'Angoulême, the Duc d'Orléans, the Queen herself—all were eager to associate their names with a factory. Under the protection of the great the porcelain industry developed with such vast strides that it is difficult even

66 The small factory of Brancas-Lauraguais produced the first hard porcelain made with kaolin quarried on French soil; a white medallion copied from a medal of Henry IV

to draw up a list of the factories which sprang into being. We must content ourselves with the principal ones.

Turgot, governor of the province of Limousin, realized immediately the profit that could accrue from the discoveries of Saint-Yrieix, in his own province. A pottery had existed at Limoges since 1736. It was directed by André Massié, architect and engineer of the Government Office of Civil Engineers. From 1770 Turgot urged Massié to change over his pottery, in which numerous experiments had been made with various clays, to porcelain manufacture. Massié therefore took as partners two wealthy Limoges men, the brothers Gillet. A chemist, Fournerat, also gave his services to the new enterprise.

Through the influence of Turgot the factory obtained, in 1773, exemption from export tax and an annual subsidy of three thousand francs to be valid for ten years, and at the same time the right to mark the porcelain C.D., for Comte d'Artois. Actually, the *vicomté* of Limoges drew revenue from the industry from 1773-1777 in favour of the future Charles X. In 1784 the King bought the Limoges factory which then became affiliated to Sèvres. It also used the Sèvres mark. Grellet still remained director, but d'Angiviller replaced him by Alluaud in 1788. On the '*18 vendemiaire an V*' during the Revolution the factory was sold to three of its former workmen.

Recently an exhibition, *Les Grands Services de Limoges*, held in the Musée A. Dubouché in Limoges in 1959, drew attention once more to this centre of the porcelain industry, which has enjoyed a considerable development from the eighteenth century up to our own day.

The first pieces appear to have been in white, then in white and gold. The multi-coloured designs of masses of mixed flowers, bouquets and garlands [plate XXVI], came later, likewise the *genre* paintings, whilst the pieces decorated with cross-hatching in gold and masses of roses appeared towards 1784.

Under the supervision of d'Angiviller and the management of Alluaud, the former white and gold and the designs 'sown' with roses in the Sèvres manner reappeared at first. But later d'Angiviller set an immediate aim for the factory, namely, to compete with Tournai. In 1788 Alluaud therefore asked Hettlinger to send him an artist capable of producing decoration of the Tournai type. Nevertheless few artists worked at Limoges. Up to 1788 there was only one; later, at least in 1790, there were three. Actually, the main work of the factory was something different—the preparation and sale of pastes ready for use by other factories. Most of the Paris factories bought their raw material there. Grellet boasts of having sold 'materials for porcelain-making' even to Copenhagen, Saint Petersburg, Amsterdam, Geneva, etc. Limoges also delivered ready-made but undecorated porcelains to other factories.

Hence, if Strasbourg played an important rôle in making known in France the processes for the manufacture of hard porcelain, Limoges contributed to their success by supplying to all who wanted it a raw material of high quality. All the hard porcelains of France are recognizable by the whiteness and the translucent quality of their paste, which was easy to mould and excluded the old danger of losing its shape in firing.

Before leaving Limousin I must mention two other porcelain centres, the one, La Seynie, situated in the province of Limousin, the other at Bordeaux, both taking their cue from the Limoges foundation.

The Marquis Beaupoil de Saint-Aulaire had devoted himself to porcelain from 1774 in his château of La Seynie, just outside Saint-Yrieix. The little factory which he established there seems to have been occupied mainly in delivering raw materials or undecorated pieces to other factories. It was bought for the Crown in 1785.

D'Angiviller, prudent administrator that he was, decided

67 The manufacture of both hard and soft porcelain continued side by side at Sèvres, where the brilliant colours typical of this factory made its work very popular for decorating furniture: a plaque from a secretaire by Weisweiler, c. 1770

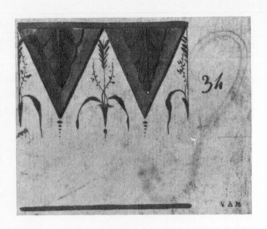

68 A sketch for a Sèvres coffee cup, *c.* 1820

that this new royal factory should specialize in the production of pieces copied from those imported from the Far East.

Two factories at least were established in Bordeaux. One of them, founded by Pierre Verneuilh, was leased to Vanier, a native of Orléans, who had worked at Lille and Valenciennes. Vanier went into partnership with Alluaud, director of the royal factory at Limoges. The presence of Alluaud, who officially only sold kaolin, explains the similarity in style between Bordeaux and Limoges porcelain. The two pieces with a design of barbels and flowers illustrated in figure 75 could equally well have come from the royal factory at Limoges.

LILLE, VALENCIENNES, ORLÉANS: Pretty well everywhere throughout the provinces hard porcelain factories began to appear—at Caen, at Chantilly founded by Monier and Pellevé, at Boissettes near Melun founded by the Vermontes, father and son, at Etiolles, at Lorient, at Bayeux, in the Landes; and the most important of all, Valenciennes, Lille and Orléans.

At Lille it was thanks to the influence of Calonne, who had already been interested in soft porcelain, that Leperre-Durot was enabled to found a factory in 1784. The furnaces were no longer fed with wood but with coal. The Dauphin having granted his protection, Lille adopted as mark a crowned dolphin. But Leperre-Durot was more interested in furnaces than in their products and his enterprise did not prosper. Having passed into other hands, it kept going until about 1815. The work had little originality, and Lille porcelain consists mainly of copies of Paris pieces.

About the same period, 1785, Fauquez of Saint-Amand obtained permission to open an establishment at Valenciennes. There he copied Sèvres and Paris pieces, but also created some original types in biscuit.

The existence of a porcelain centre at Orléans has

69 The Bourbon family were generous and enthusiastic patrons of many porcelain factories. The Comte d'Artois, later Charles X, was the protector of the Faubourg Saint-Denis enterprise from 1779 until the Revolution. This tureen dates from this period of manufacture

70 With the discovery of kaolin in France, new hard paste porcelain factories sprang up. These two pieces were produced by Robert's factory at Marseilles

71 This covered cup and saucer were produced at Orléans, under Sèvres influence

72 A sketch for a Sèvres coffee cup, *c.* 1820

already been mentioned. Its director Gérault changed over to the production of hard porcelain. Just as he had done in Marseilles, Monsieur, the King's eldest brother, honoured this factory also with a visit in 1777. That day there were displayed in the factory showroom '24,000 fancy flowers in open boxes on the counter, quantities of semi-natural flowers in white, natural flowers of all kinds, painted... 295 groups of different heights... 750 figures of all sizes, pieces for use and for ornament in colours and gilded... The greater part of the sculptures in biscuit', (Chavagnac and Grollier). Flowers and biscuit figures were far from representing the whole of the Orléans production. Charming polychrome pieces of the type shown in figure 71, often influenced by Sèvres, Paris or Tournai, bear the mark of the factory, which was the label which figures in the arms of the Orléans family.

SÈVRES AND THE PARIS FACTORIES: Sèvres, immediately after the discovery of kaolin deposits at Saint-Yrieix, set about buying a territory to quarry, and their chemist Macquer had made numerous experiments. The production of hard porcelain, which did not oust the soft porcelain, was taken up systematically from 1772. It is not always easy to distinguish the pieces from the royal factory executed in soft paste from those in hard paste—the same artists worked on both the moulds and the decoration. The table services delivered by the factory often consisted of both soft and hard porcelains.

The mark of the hard pastes is almost the same as that of the soft ones, but on the latter a closed crown surmounts the two interlaced L's which accompany the letter denoting date. The first of the letters denoting dates was U for 1769. The letters are doubled from 1778 onwards.

73 Yet another Bourbon, the Duc d'Angoulême (son of the Comte d'Artois), was patron of the rue de Bondy factory, managed by Dihl and Guerhard from 1781-96. This beautiful teapot was made during their partnership

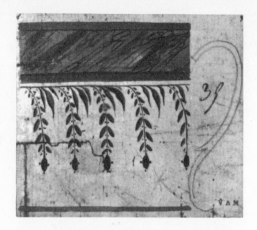

74 An early nineteenth-century design for a Sèvres coffee cup

The ease of firing from now onwards enabled Sèvres not only to continue the manufacture of biscuit but also to launch out on larger compositions. Side by side with table services supplied by the factory, pieces of exceptional size were baked. D'Angiviller was personally interested in the making of large vases mounted in ormolu. In 1783 Hettlinger made out a detailed account for him, describing the work which these required. The great vase of the Louvre is no less than six and a half feet high—a marvellous technical feat [plate XXII]. It was commissioned by the King in 1783 and bears the signatures of the sculptor Boizot and of the bronze-smith Thomire. Less important, but executed with the same deep blue ground and in the same manner, is another vase to which the date 1787 can be given [figure 81]. Similar vases were delivered to Versailles for the Cabinet of the Council that same year.

The making of great vases was not to cease with the eighteenth century. From the Empire to the Third Republic the factory continued to create models which, though sometimes in dubious taste, always display the same masterly workmanship.

It is not my task to follow the fortunes of Sèvres far into the nineteenth century; nevertheless the continuity of production of the Imperial factory, as reformed by Alexandre Brongniart, can be seen from two examples illustrated here.

The Egyptian Tea Service [plates XXXII, XXXIII] was delivered to Napoleon on the 31st March 1810. In the beginning it consisted of twenty-four cups and saucers, one Etruscan sugar bowl, two other bowls of the kind known as *pestum* (pestle) for sugar and two milk jugs. The superb gilding was carried out by Micaud and Legrand, and the paintings by Robert, Lebel and Béranger. Micaud and Legrand had already been in the service of the factory in the previous century; the three other were newcomers. The subjects are taken from *Voyage dans la Basse et Haute*

XXVI Limoges was one of the many factories which came into existence with the discovery of kaolin in France: this cup and saucer bears the arms of the de Mesmes family

75 The products of the Limoges and Bordeaux factories were remarkably similar and these pieces could equally well have come from either factory. They are, in fact, from Bordeaux

Egypte (1802) by Vivant Denon. The novel and the traditional are felicitously blended in this work. The other example is shown in plate XXXIV, and is part of the '*Service Iconographique Italien*' delivered to the Emperor in 1814. The tradition of the great table services was by no means lost: it has continued into our own day.

At the end of the eighteenth century all the Paris hard porcelains had several traits in common—the perfectly vitrified quality of the paste, its brilliant whiteness, and the completely legible design, of which the forms and modes of expression were often inspired by Sèvres. The biscuit pieces were still highly esteemed, as were also the little pictures and the vases of all shapes. The accent was on utility, and the production comprised more tableware than works of art or collectors' pieces. The porcelains of the end of the eighteenth century were no longer, properly speaking, original creations. Here as elsewhere technical perfection had inaugurated an era of ease of production which did not favour artistic creation.

Among the innovations one should note, nevertheless, the interesting process which was only patented in 1810 but which Nast had been using earlier in the factory in the rue Popincourt which he had bought in 1783, and then transferred to the Rue des Amandiers-Popincourt. This patent covered 'a process for making raised mouldings'. It is not at all clear, on the other hand, what were the processes for printing on porcelain which the Englishman Potter used so extensively.

The designs of butterflies [plate XXVIII] and chequered borders of the Petit-Carrousel factory also deserve mention as innovations. For *genre* paintings, figures, wreaths of flowers all too often give an impression of outmodedness which was to be overcome to some extent at the beginning of the nineteenth century, at least in the case of those firms which had survived the revolutionary period.

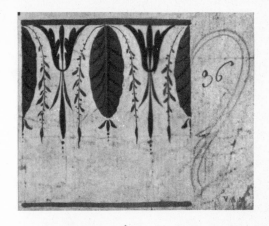

76 An early nineteenth-century design for a Sèvres coffee cup

115

XXVII A teapot and cup and saucer from Marie Antoinette's dressing-case which was ordered 'to serve in case of sudden flight', from the rue Amelot works patronised by Philippe-Egalité

XXVIII A ewer and basin from the factory in the rue Petit-Carrousel, which may perhaps have been only a workshop for decorating manufactured pieces

The porcelains of Clignancourt are generally referred to as 'Les Porcelaines de Monsieur'; nevertheless it was not until 1775 that the firm of Deruelle, which had already been in existence four years, was granted the patronage of the future Louis XVIII. Before adopting the monogram of the King's brother in 1775, Deruelle used as mark a more or less stylized representation of the windmill adjoining his factory. The enterprise was an important one. In 1786 ninety-four workers were employed there and actually ten years before that the directors of Sèvres were worried by its activity, which was competing seriously with theirs and seducing their workers, for their royal protector assured them relative impunity. Deruelle's son-in-law Moitte succeeded him as director, and Clignancourt continued in production until the end of the century. The ewer and basin shown in figure 80 bear the windmill mark, hence they are earlier than 1775. The whiteness of the paste, the brilliance of the gilding, the medallions inspired by *genre* paintings in the fashion of the time, are all characteristic of Clignancourt.

The Comte d'Artois, later Charles X, like his brother, accorded his patronage in 1779 to a new enterprise. It was the Faubourg Saint-Denis factory, established eight years previously by the notorious Pierre-Antoine Hannong, its mark, two pipes, being no doubt in memory of the family's first factory at Strasbourg. The table pieces bear gilded ornaments, and landscapes are not infrequent. Some with garlands [figure 69] marked CP surmounted by a crown, are reminiscent of Limoges porcelain which had enjoyed the same royal patronage at one time. In 1798 Marc Schoelcher, better known as a politician than as a porcelain manufacturer, took over the Faubourg Saint-Denis factory, and his advent ushered in a considerable period of renewed activity.

78 A cup and saucer from Locré's factory in Paris, showing how the simple *chinoiserie* decoration of the early French pieces has become entirely European in expression

77 A Sèvres plaque in soft paste used to decorate a drop-front secretaire, 1766

119

XXIX A plate from the *Service des Asturies*, Sèvres, 1789 decorated with landscapes and garlands

XXXI A plate from the *Service Iconographique Italien* delivered to Napoleon from Sèvres in 1814, decorated with a portrait of Andrea del Sarto. Inscribed on the back is a brief description of this painter

XXX A Sèvres cup and saucer with a violet ground and Chinese figures, 1783

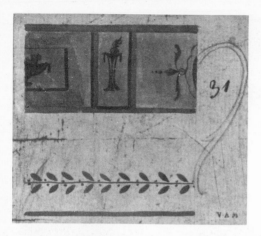

79 An early nineteenth-century sketch for
a Sèvres coffee cup

The Orléans family, too, took an interest in the porcelain-
industry throughout the eighteenth century. We have
seen how the Regent confided a trade secret to Henri
Trou. His grandson Louis-Philippe, patron of scholars
and men of letters, sponsored experiments in his château
at Bagnolet. It was he who protected the manufacture
at Boissettes. It was also he who had permitted Pierre-
Antoine Hannong to set up at Vincennes. The future Philippe-Egalité granted his patronage in 1786 to
Outrequin de Montarcy, porcelain manufacturer, of the
Rue Amelot. The letters L.P. (Louis-Philippe) appear on
certain porcelains sometimes attributed to Vincennes,
sometimes to the Rue Amelot, which is believed to have
also used the monogram MO, variously interpreted as
Manufacture d'Orléans, or Outrequin-Montarcy, or Or-
léans-Montarcy.

This monogram figures on the porcelain fittings of the
dressing-case of Marie Antoinette [plate XXVII] which
had been ordered 'to serve in case of sudden flight', as
Madame Campan wrote. On the eve of her flight to Var-
ennes the Queen appears to have ordered her porcelains
from a factory whose patron, Philippe-Egalité, was one of
her worst enemies, who afterwards voted for the death of
the King before dying by the guillotine himself.

All the Paris porcelain works, and some of the provincial
ones too, had their warehouses and retail merchants in
Paris. The Clignancourt porcelains were obtainable from
Monsieur de la Fresnaye at the Palais-Royal, those of the
Comte d'Artois at the factory itself in the Faubourg
Saint-Denis, and also from Bailleux, Faubourg Saint-
Germain, and Leduc, Rue des Échelles at the corner of the
Rue du Petit-Carrousel. Leduc also sold porcelains marked
with an A surmounted by a crown, and decorated in the
Sèvres style with sprays of multi-coloured flowers or
various emblems. The same goods were retailed by Gran-

80 A ewer and basin from the Paris factory at Clignancourt, *c.* 1771-75

XXXII Part of the famous Egyptian Tea Service made for Napoleon,
painted with scenes from Denon's *Voyage dans la Basse et Haute Egypte*
and gilded with Egyptian hieroglyphics, Sèvres, 1810

XXXIII One of the
two milk jugs from
the Egyptian Tea
Service. Napoleon's
expedition to the
Nile inspired the first
interest in Egypt-
ology among Euro-
pean scholars

chez, quai de Conti, at the sign of the *Petit-Dunkerque*. They were manufactured in the Rue Thiroux and were called '*porcelaines à la Reine*'. This factory was run by one Lebeuf who, because of disputes with Sèvres, was obliged to close down temporarily in 1787, in spite of the high patronage which he enjoyed.

At Rue du Petit-Carrousel Guy, the successor of Leduc, not content with retailing manufactured products, went into production himself, but his workshop may have been only a centre for decorating manufactured pieces, often in original designs [plate XXVIII].

At the Rue Fontaine-au-Roy one Locré, himself also a porcelain maker, carried on a business which does not seem always to have been entirely honest. Copies of Sèvres, table-ware or biscuit figures, were numerous. The cup decorated with pictures of Chinese figures, now in the Musée de Sèvres, bears his mark—two crossed torches [figure 78]. A mark deliberately similar (two crossed arrows) is attributed to a little factory which was situated in the Rue de la Roquette in the old Hôtel des Arbalétriers (hence the arrows?), at the sign of the *Trois Levrettes*.

Finally, there is the Rue de Bondy foundation. Here we find another member of the Royal Family, the Duc d'Angoulême, son of the Comte d'Artois, as protector of one of the most important Paris manufactures of porcelain. Dihl and Guerhard, who ran it, had been in partnership since 1781. They profited considerably by the relaxation of the monopoly of Sèvres, a relaxation which they had helped to bring about. Marked with the monogram G. A. (Guerhard-Angoulême), their porcelains are always of perfect workmanship. The dissolution of the firm in 1829 was followed by a sale of which the mere announcement suffices to give an indication of the objects sold—'vases,

82 An early nineteenth-century design for a Sèvres coffee cup

81 A large vase mounted in ormolu with a deep blue ground, typical of the ambitious pieces of hard paste porcelain made at Sèvres, *c.* 1787

127

dinner services, tea services, lunch services of every shape and size, some with coloured ground, painted and gilded, others with coloured ground only, and others in plain white'. In 1796 Dihl and Guerhard changed to the Rue du Temple. It is interesting to compare the teapot in the Musée de Sèvres [figure 73] with the one in Marie Antoinette's *nécessaire*; the frieze of pansies in green, blue, yellow, red and violet are of an exquisite delicacy.

The beauty and perfection of this piece would alone suffice to prove that the best porcelain makers at the end of the century had not abandoned the traditions which had won their predecessors such high renown.

XXXIV A Sèvres plate with a tortoise-shell ground, decorated with a blue-headed parrot from Guiana, 1792